Pedaling Northwards

A Father and Son's
Bicycle Adventure
from
Virginia to Canada

Robin Lind

HOPE SPRINGS PRESS

MANAKIN-SABOT, VIRGINIA

1993

Printed in the United States of America
First Edition

ISBN 0-9639531-0-9

Portions of this work originally appeared in the Richmond Times-Dispatch
and on daily broadcasts of WCVE-FM, Richmond, Virginia.

for Kitty

Randy—
Here's something
you could do!
Keep biking—
Love,
Mom + Dad

Dec. 30, 1995

Pedaling Northwards

PEDALING NORTHWARDS OUT OF CULPEPER on Rt. 229
at a steady 12 miles an hour, my son and I turned
right at Catalpa onto Rt. 625 and headed northeast toward Warrenton. A group of young boys hanging
off a porch at the lonely house on the corner yelled to us as
we went by and one of them jumped onto a small bike and
pedaled furiously after us, his crew-cut head bobbing up
and down as he tried to catch up.

"Where're you goin'?" he shouted.

"Canada," I called back over my shoulder.

"Naw. Where're you goin'?"

"Canada," I repeated.

"Naw. Really. Where're you headed?" he panted, legs
furiously pumping the little bike after us.

"Canada. We're really biking to Canada," I yelled back
to him.

He slowed and stopped. Stood astride the small bike
and looked after us in either disbelief or disgust. I suppose
he thought we were just pulling his leg. (Grown-ups will
do that to you sometimes).

The road curved and dipped as we pushed into three-
rail fenced horse and cattle country. I couldn't see him any-
more. He couldn't see us. But then again, we had been

there. He had seen us himself. Heavy man with full beard, sweat-soaked T-shirt and shorts, yellow helmet, dark glasses, big blue bike with overstuffed blue saddlebags and a sweat-soaked teenager with a glossy black helmet, similarly overstuffed blue saddlebags.

It didn't seem so at the time but, as I think back, that little incident was a defining moment for us on the trip.

We were on the second day of our bicycle trip from Richmond to Canada and it really began to sink in that ours was not a commonplace vacation. My son and I had biked as much as 90 miles on day trips in the past but we had never attempted a long distance adventure like this. Although I had biked through Portugal, Spain and France with a pal from school a quarter of a century ago, that was long ago and far away and I hadn't done anything like it in the intervening years. It took a small boy on the outskirts of Culpeper to give us a different sense of perspective.

I don't know where he thought Canada was. Perhaps Canada as a destination was to him as foreign a place as the Moon. Certainly it is a foreign country and it is a fair piece away from rural Virginia. Still, it's not as far as Florida — but most Virginians such have a vague impression of geography as to be highly doubtful when you tell them that Fairfax is closer to New York City than it is to Bristol, Virginia.

I think what troubled the boy was the concept that anyone could propel himself so far from home that he couldn't return home by dark. It's not something we're familiar with. Bicycling is something for children. It's something for fun and sport. It's short-range. It's a lark.

It's also a wonderful way to see America. It's a way to get away from it all by getting just about as close to it all as you can get.

When you're bicycling you have a lot of time to think alone. You can ride in company with someone else but you can't ride alongside — that's not safe. So you ride one after another and chat only when you halt for rest and water. Sometimes you don't even chat then. The hills wear you down. The constant pedaling becomes mechanical. You get your second wind. Your brain fills with endorphins — you experience "the runner's high" — and you forget about aches and pains and exhaustion.

You have a chance to study the distant mountains, the way the clouds play on them. You notice the change in scent as you leave the towns and cities and automobile exhaust and smell the fresh mown hay, new silage, cattle and horse manure. You feel the sun on your back and the breeze on your face. When you're headed north you judge the time of day by whether your shadow falls on the roadbank on your right or your left. You search out the shade at the top of a hill so you can pull over and rest up a bit without being roasted in the noonday sun. Most of all, you just push on.

By the end of that second day we would be in Warrenton. We would have covered 44 miles of hilly rural Piedmont since leaving Rapidan. We crossed Muddy Run, the Hazel River, Beaverdam Run, the Rappahannock River, Barrows Run, Great Run (twice) and several unnamed branches and creeks. I came into Warrenton on the Fauquier Springs Road pushing my bike up the last cruel hill, wondering if I could possibly survive another 10 minutes let alone another 10 days. My 15-year-old son Frank was waiting at the top: "Good work, Dad!" and so I went on.

When you bike through a countryside you really get to know it. You also learn skills of the road:

- never, never run low on water;
- always ask where the next bike shop is in case you need help;
- avoid big highways, with their constant stream of 18-wheelers, like the plague but be grateful for the professional drivers on those big rigs who will give you much more room on the road than an expense-account salesman with a big sedan and a car phone in his ear;
- make sure you have a detailed map; check the local landmarks on your map as well as the roadsigns: rural humorists still delight in switching the signposts but they can't move a creek or shift a power line;
- don't expect the natives to know about local or nearby points of interest; after all, they live here and have never felt a need to go touring;
- find a road that parallels a railroad track, a canal or a river: it's very likely flat, or at least on a gentler grade than the one that crosses all those runs, branches, creeks, and rivers.

When people ask — still incredulously — *how* we did it, we have to say, well it was just one day at a time. Manakin to Rapidan, Rapidan to Warrenton, Warrenton to Leesburg and across the Potomac into Maryland and up to Frederick, from Frederick into Pennsylvania to Gettysburg and on to Harrisburg, crossed the Susquehanna River and up to Shamokin Dam, from Shamokin Dam to Williamsport and

Trout Run, Trout Run up the Lycoming Valley into New York State to Elmira, Elmira to Watkins Glen and up past Seneca Lake to Rose, from Rose to Sodus Point on Lake Ontario and then west to Rochester, from Rochester to Niagara and then we were in Canada.

When people ask — still more incredulously — *why* we did it, well, that's more difficult to answer. There is a simple answer, of course. My family moved to Canada from King George County back in 1952 and my parents still live there. For more than 20 years we embarked on annual pilgrimages, returning to Virginia to visit my mother's family. For the past 20 years, since I moved to Virginia, many of the pilgrimages have gone the other way. Before the construction of modern roads (and the availability of automobile air conditioning), the trip took two days. In recent years it has been reduced to about 12 hours of high speed — if monotonous — cruising on Interstates.

There's also a more complex answer. Sometimes you need to seize the moment. Sometimes you need to venture into the unknown. Sometimes you need to take a literal journey of faith to symbolize the metaphysical journey of faith that is our daily existence. Sometimes you just need to stretch yourself physically and psychologically to get the kinks out.

I am firmly convinced that life is, and ought to be, an adventure. For the most part, we travel the paths of least resistance. Having faced countless hills (up-hills and down-hills) on this bicycle trip I am all in favor of the downward path but I have immense respect for those who travel up-hill, even those who get off and walk and push their load ahead of them: they are still moving forward. They are still pushing themselves onward. They are putting in whatever effort is required to reach the point where they'll have the reward of a glorious, breezy, exhilarating downhill.

It's great exercise. It's a grand weight-loss program. It may even hold a metaphor for life.

Our story could be your story. You don't have to follow our route. You might be headed in the opposite direction. But if you plan your trip and take sensible precautions you'll find a an extraordinary adventure unfolding before you.

In the following pages, even those who don't plan to pedal their way to Canada can ride with us and enjoy some of the scenery along the way. More and more people are taking up bicycling and one of the major changes over the past quarter century has been the major increase in courtesy and indulgence toward cyclists on the part of motorists who find them sharing the roads.

Thank you for that. Please keep it up.

*A Father and Son's
Bicycle Adventure
from
Virginia to Canada*

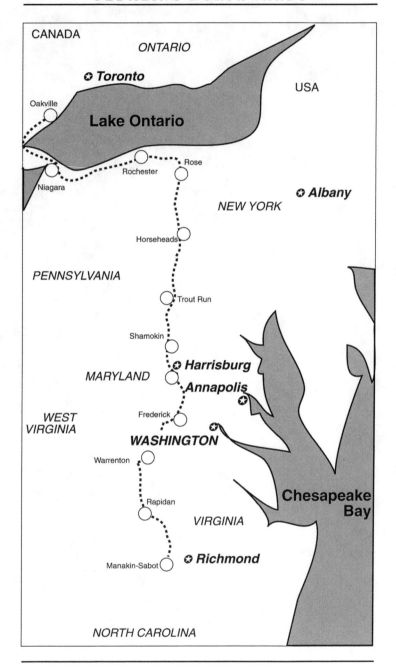

SETTING OUT

W E BEGIN OUR VIRGINIA TO CANADA bicycle trip from our own back yard in Manakin-Sabot, about 18 miles west of Richmond. Our home is on the edge of the old Boscobel Ferry Road which leads down to the James River. We're about 12 miles above the "fall line" where the earliest settlers found the rivers blocked by rocks — the "falls" that became the first natural settlements at Richmond, Fredericksburg and Washington.

According to Swiss explorer John Lederer who passed through in 1670, our area was already the site of a large Indian Village that had been peopled by a tribe led by a Chieftain named Manak — a visionary leader who had led his people out of the upper Shenandoah during a time of starvation and found the rich bottom lands of the James River Valley. Thirty years later it was settled by French Protestants — the Huguenots — who named an island in the James for its appearance like a shoe.

Although it has been rural for the past three hundred years, the east end of our county is rapidly filling up with Richmond office workers who daily commute to and from the capital. Our community (with the only double-barrelled name in Virginia) is a result of a compromise combining the two nearby post offices.

Our planned route will take us past two golf courses and several upscale subdivisions, over Interstate 64, past more modern housing developments before we get into a patchwork of hobby farms and abandoned fields awaiting final "best possible use."

Over the course of several days we've checked and rechecked our gear, cleaned our bikes and oiled them. I reckon we've made them as roadworthy as possible considering my bike is a 21-year-old Italian racer which I got in college and my son's is a 5-year-old Schwinn he inherited from my brother.

I've got 10 gears. He's got 18.

I'm carrying 200 pounds. He's carrying 120. That doesn't count the 50 to 60 pounds of gear each of us has loaded on the big blue nylon saddle bags mounted on the bikes. We have packed our gear in Zip-Loc bags to protect them from rain — a neat compartmentalization that gives us each day's clean clothes in a separate baggie.

We carry three water bottles apiece — filled with Gatorade we've mixed at home. We have bed rolls and rain ponchos that will double as groundsheets. We wear cotton T-shirts and shorts, ordinary tennis shoes. No fancy black nylon girdles with neon sponsor logos for us. This is no Tour duPont: this is a Tour de Rump.

We carry a half-dozen expensive energy bars apiece that are supposed to provide concentrated energy as a sort of survival kit in case we're stuck somewhere without food. We have abandoned our mess tins and cooking gear because of the extra weight. We expect to live off the land, so to speak — as long as we're traveling in the land of fast food restaurants and local cafés.

Over the next two weeks we expect to be sweating our way north through Piedmont Virginia, into western Maryland, on over the mountains of Pennsylvania, up into the Finger Lakes of New York all the way to the shores of Lake Ontario. There we plan to turn left and head for Niagara. Cross the river and we're there: in Canada.

It is to be an adventure.

My son is 15. Next year he'll be old enough to drive and the adventure of traveling anywhere by bike will probably lose some of its appeal.

I'm 43. The last time I ventured out on a bicycle like this I was 18. That's a quarter of a century ago. People ask what we've done to train for this exertion and I tell them I've been resting up to conserve my strength. (After 25 years it ought to be conserved enough.)

I had forgotten the pain of waking in the night with a cyclist's charley horse but one of my younger brothers has been kind enough to remind me. He thinks I'm intrepid.

My sister is one of several who looks at the map and suggests we should start in Canada and then bike south so it would all be downhill. She thinks I'm low on humor.

The rest of my family is fairly certain I'm crazy.

But my wife is a fount of understanding. She understands she can't *dis*-suade us so she patiently tries to *per*-suade us.

Per-suade us to go easy. Quit when it gets to hot. Ride in the cool of the day. Be willing to call a halt even if we haven't reached our destination. Drink plenty of fluids. Stay off the main roads. Get plenty of rest. Don't be afraid to call for her to come pick us up. And, whatever else, always wear a helmet — she doesn't want to spend the rest of her life taking care of a simpleton. (I'm so charmed at the implied compliment that I readily agree).

Everyone offers advice. No one offers to join us.

The heat of a Virginia summer morn is a formidable launching pad but we're finally ready to launch. We've delayed our start for three days as the thermometer has sunk into the 80s overnight and risen quickly back into the high 90s and inched over 100 every afternoon. Finally the weather forecasters predict a break in the heat and we decide it's now or never.

The dogs are put inside so they won't follow us and the kitchen door slams one last time behind us. We switch on the pale beams of our headlights in the pre-dawn grayness, adjust our helmets, mount the bikes and slip our shoes into the toe clips.

We're off.

My wife waves good-bye and our 13-year-old daughter Maria pulls away with us as an escort for the first four miles. She has caught the sense of excitement that comes with the start of an adventure — but she is not about to get so excited as to want to join us for the whole trip.

Our route will take us from our home up the Hermitage Road to Centerville on Rt. 250 where Maria will bid us farewell. Then we will pedal north on the Manakin Road, over I-64, where early-morning commuters are already filling the road and squinting into the dawn on their way into Richmond. North to Rockville, to Oticon, cross the South Anna River, up to Montpelier, along the Helltown Road to the Shiloh Church Road, up the Woodson Mill Road to

Belches Road to Buckner and then onto the Lake Anna Road and over to Dickinson's Store on Rt. 522. Cross Rt. 522 and we'll head onto the Ellisville Road up to Monrovia, Orange and finally to Rapidan.

We have driven this route once and have a fair idea of what we'll encounter. It's all rural countryside. No heavy traffic. No mean hills. And the stretch along Lake Anna is flat and encouraging. Today we want to cover 75 miles — 60 miles before noon if we can manage it.

This is our way of gently edging into the regimen of daily cycling.

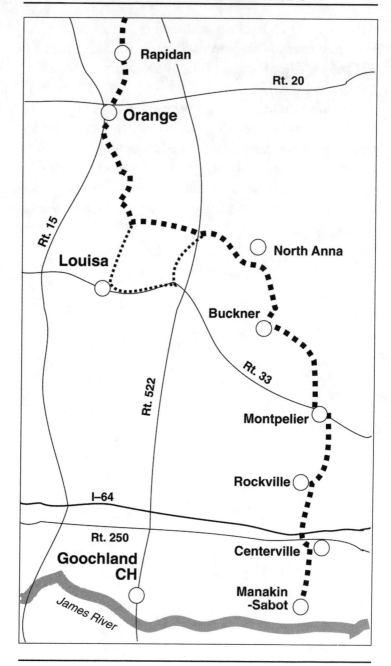

DAY 1
MANAKIN-SABOT TO RAPIDAN

W E HAVE MADE IT to our first destination: the little village of Rapidan, straddling the Orange and Culpeper County lines.
Yesterday we headed north-northwest through Goochland, Hanover, Louisa and Orange Counties. It was smooth riding and pretty easy going most of the way: after all, we reached Dickinson's Store on Rt. 522 just west of Lake Anna Nuclear Power Plant by lunch time and that's pretty good cycling if you ask me.

Pretty easy too, if you don't count the blowout I had at mile four just as the sun came up. The 12-year-old rear tire couldn't stand the extra weight and just gave out. I thought I felt an unusual squishy-ness under me about mile three and by the time the bike had begun to wobble more than it should have, the dawn had brightened enough to let me see the black inner tube swelling through the ruptured sidewall.

This was, you might say, unexpected. It was good practice though: loosen the quick release hub lever; drop off the wheel; strip off the old tubular tire, glue on the spare; pump it up; note with interest the way in which the 10-year-old air pump comes irreparably apart in my hands;

borrow my son's pump; get the new tire inflated hard as a rock; reassemble the wheel and pose for a photograph taken by my daughter. (Broad Street Road is as far as she intends to go on our trip and I give her the blown tire and broken pump as souvenirs — souvenirs that I later discovered would fill my wife with horror and foreboding).

Being a responsible father though, I cheerfully laughed off the inconvenience and told my son that this was exactly why I had brought two spare tires in the first place. This was part of the adventure! We should be grateful for such an experience so early on.

And so we bid Maria farewell, crossed Rt. 250 as the first commuters began to appear on the road, and pedaled north past the drought-stunted corn rows of eastern Goochland.

We covered 85.4 miles on our first day — a little farther than we planned after our maps fell out of my pocket as I strained up some nameless hill somewhere south of Montpelier. I had the maps when we stopped at Woodson's Mill on Little River but they were gone when we got to Rt. 33.

Turn back? Loose valuable time? Create unnecessary double mileage? Use up precious energy? Risk missing our destination before nightfall? They could be only a hundred yards back or five miles. Could we make do without?

I ran all the alternatives through my mind and decided we would do without. One of my kinsmen had recommended this route and in previous years had marked the road with blue spray-painted arrows at critical junctions to guide his own children biking from Richmond to Rapidan;

most of the arrows are still faintly visible and we've already seen the first. We'd go ahead without the maps.

My confidence rose as we moved steadily ahead, spotting the faint blue arrows. I'm pleased that I had been able to adjust to circumstances so easily but it is an early confidence that was sorely shaken when we paid a surprise visit to Louisa Court House.

I knew something was amiss when we didn't find the turnoff for the Ellisville Road after crossing Rt. 522. There were turnoffs, of course, but they weren't marked with road signs and we couldn't see any paint. Without the map to guide us I was looking for an intersection only dimly-remembered from the car trip several weeks earlier.

We were hot and drenched with sweat, consuming a pint of Gatorade every half hour. Every time I looked down at the main gear sprockets below me a rivulet of sweat ran from my chin, where it had collected at the helmet strap, and splashed on the crossbar. There was a constant need to replenish our water supply and we were going through an unfamiliar stretch of Louisa that was almost uninhabited.

Down to my last half pint on an empty road near Duckinghoe Creek I spied two men working on a tractor near an isolated old garage and stopped to see if they had a water spigot.

"You want drinking water?" one replied.

"Yes, just to refill our water bottles," I answered.

"Well, we ain't got no water spigot but I got a gallon jug I carry with me and I'd be willing to divide with you."

I was a total stranger, soaked with sweat, wearing a yellow helmet my daughter says makes me look like "the king of dorks," riding an overladen bike on one of the hottest and most humid days of the summer, on the side of an almost deserted country road, near no place of habitation, but he was still willing to share what little he had. I was touched beyond measure ... the words that sprang to mind came straight out of Matthew 25: "I was thirsty and ye gave me drink ..." Perhaps there was a purpose in our losing our way.

When we hit Rt. 22-208 halfway between Mineral and Louisa C.H. I realized we had made a major error. With the sun completely obscured by heat haze I didn't even know which direction we were heading and had to ask directions from a couple of linemen stringing Cable TV line across the road.

Going ten miles the wrong way in a car is scarcely anything to get worked up about nowadays but when you're biking it means you've wasted critical resources, and two hours of critical daylight that have to be made up before you reach your destination. The knowledge comes like a body-blow in an 11th-round boxing match that almost knocks you down. You can't just turn around and go back. You can't give up. You have to take it, roll with the punch, and keep going.

We pedaled into Louisa Court House and asked directions of a construction worker laying new asphalt on Main Street and he advised us to go back the way we'd come.

"But doesn't this road lead to Gordonsville and Orange?" I asked.

"Don't know," he answered, "Never been down that road. But you can get to Orange County by going back the way you came."

I concluded that I still have a natural ability — akin to the natural forces of gravity — to attract the one individual in a crowd who has absolutely no information and even less natural intelligence. Then I had to remind myself that I was the one who was lost, not him — and I was the one bicycling through the unfamiliar countryside in 95-degree heat with no maps.

We headed on through town and got new directions onto the Ellisville Road which led us to the old Monrovia Highway into Orange. Out of Louisa we crossed Gold Mine, Chaney, Nunn and Humphrey Creeks and I learned one of the long-distance cyclist's major lessons: rural roads that cross creeks have hills. Hills that go down are always followed by hills that go up. Hills that go up, I reminded myself — as I got off to walk and push — are not my idea of fun.

I can manage low rises and slow climbs. I can even manage a few stiff inclines when I'm fresh. But after 60 miles I've about had it. After 75 miles the novelty has worn thin. I can walk uphill at 3 miles per hour. The struggle of pushing the pedals around at 4 miles per hour just isn't worth it, even if I had the stamina to do it.

We came into Orange in late afternoon weary but determined.

Determined to complete this first leg of the journey but too weary to stop and study the stone marker that commemorates the Grand Inspection of the Army of Northern Virginia by President Jefferson Davis on the great meadow northeast of town. History would have to wait for further examination on another trip.

Frank, with his extra gears, lighter weight — and the fitness and energy of youth — has patiently waited for me at the summit of each successive hill and now paces himself to let me keep up. But even he has his limits.

Just a few miles short of our destination in Rapidan I see him suddenly wobble and then pitch sideways on the road, 50 yards ahead of me. His front wheel has fallen off the edge of the pavement on one of Virginia's most attractive rural roads that boasts little traffic but absolutely no shoulder. In trying to recover he has been thrown headlong onto the road, instantly rasping skin from forearm, elbow, wrist, thigh, knee and ankle.

It is a frightening sight to see anyone go down in the road. Terrifying when it's your own child. You want to reach out and catch him but you can't. You're too far away. Your adrenaline surges and you race forward. You skid to a halt and leap off your bike. Blood is already oozing over the surface where his skin has been chafed off.

Praise God he's all right. No broken bones. No concussion. Only surface abrasions.

His helmet has protected his head. The absence of traffic has saved his life. The lesson is obvious to both of us: anyone can become careless after more than 80 miles of biking in unrelenting heat.

We vow to be more careful — and carry on.

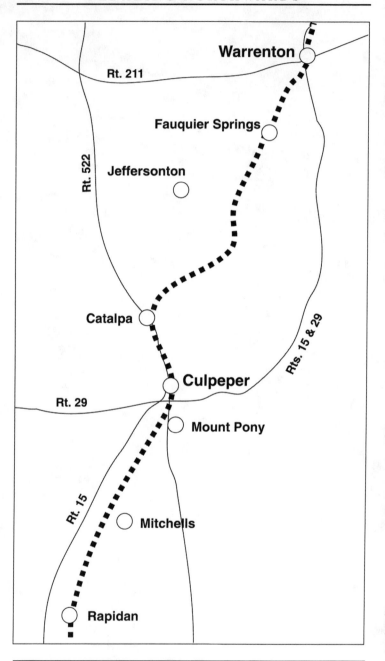

DAY 2
RAPIDAN TO WARRENTON

YESTERDAY WE STARTED OUT with a nice steady pace on a straight level road parallel to the Southern Railroad track running northeast from Rapidan. The sun was coming up over Clark's Mountain and the Blue Ridge was faintly visible in the haze to the west. This was the what I had in mind when we set out. A steady, easy pace at about 12 miles per hour across level farmland with no traffic and the open road to ourselves.

Then another blowout at mile four. What is it about mile four?

My dear old narrow racing tires don't seem to be holding up to this kind of pace. This was the brand new tire I put on yesterday and already the sidewall has worn through.

We change tires, install the remaining spare and shift course for Culpeper where we'd been told there's a bike store that can supply some more spares and maybe a new chain to replace mine which has begun to stretch.

The change in plans also gives us the excuse to stop in at the Dominion Wine Cellars Co-Op near Mount Pony. "After all," my wife advised us before we set out, "this isn't supposed to be a reenactment of the Bataan Death March; enjoy yourselves."

So we did. Wanda Holloway gave us our own personal tour of the operation which processes the grapes produced by almost two dozen local vineyards, including the welcome opportunity to stand beside the 20,000-gallon cooling tanks covered with a thick white blanket of frost. I refrained from the wide selection of tastings only with the greatest of reluctance: I don't know if the police can pick up a cyclist for driving under the influence but I know for darn sure that alcohol and hot sun and strenuous pedaling can be a lethal combination — helmet or no helmet.

On to Culpeper where we quickly found the bike shop and I got the last spare tubular tire they had in stock and a new chain to replace the old. The new chain doesn't seem to fit quite properly and I soon find that I can't shift into top gear but I decide to press on anyway. I reckon it will sort itself out or I can adjust it later when we get out on the road.

So it's north on the Catalpa Road onto the Alanthus Road and up towards Fauquier Springs. I halt for a rest at a shady hedgerow, prop my bicycle on its kick stand and watch curiously as it slowly falls into the ditch. When I wrestle it upright, the weight over the rear tire nearly overbalances me. I see that the old cast-aluminum kick stand has fractured and broken. Well, I tell Frank, that's another couple of ounces of relic that I won't have to carry with me all the way to Canada; and I contribute the metal stake to the barbed-wire fence line.

The Blue Ridge is an unending line of rumpled, hazy blue mountains stretching along our left with rolling hills in forest and pasture reaching up to meet them about eight miles away. Three panel fences crisscross the landscape. The road is narrow but fairly smooth pavement. There's no shoulder of course and mostly a one to three foot ditch. Roadside fences are overgrown and scraggly trees give us some patchy shelter from the sun. Cattle and horses stand motionless in whatever shade they can find. Small worn-out old frame houses, many abandoned, mark the passing of old communities; modern brick bungalows, close to the road but far apart from each other, mark the creation of the new; huge oaks and poplars lean over large old houses at the end of tree-lined avenues in the distance, marking the continuing popularity of the agrarian tradition even as the people continue to leave the land.

I tell Frank we have picked this route because we need to worry more about trucks than about hills but by the time we have gone up and down, and up and down, and up and down, and I finally walk across the town line into Warrenton, pushing my bike up the last hill heaving and blowing, I begin to question my own judgment. If I have to keep facing hills in this heat I'm going to be dead anyway — trucks or no trucks. I'll be hill-kill, not road-kill.

We stop in the shade at the Court House in Warrenton and rest at the feet of a statue of Chief Justice John Marshall who was born and raised in Fauquier County. I wonder what the famous jurist — now claimed by Historic Richmond as one its most distinguished former residents — would have said of our adventure. The only choice he had in his day was foot, horseback, wagon or boat. I don't think he would have been at all surprised at the thought of our riding from Richmond to Warrenton.

James Timberlake, a local businessman, spying our bikes against the tree, comes over to chat. He owns the local paint store. I ask how long he's been in business in Warrenton.

"Five generations," he answers.

People take the long view out here in the countryside. I expect that means he might have sold paint to John Marshall if John Marshall had bought any paint. At least *his* people might have traded with *his* people. There's a sense of belonging.

James explains he's a cyclist himself and plans to go out tomorrow morning at dawn to ride up to Little Washington in Rappahannock County and be back before breakfast. He's not trying to get anywhere; it's just for the exercise.

I'm about to tell him my conclusion about hills and traffic but then I realize he's going to have both trucks and hills on Rt. 211 going up to Little Washington. He's probably done it before. From the looks of him, he probably does it regularly. I keep my own counsel and give a nod to the Chief Justice.

The spectacular views of Virginia's rolling Piedmont take on a new perspective when viewed from the saddle — they've even more sharply focused from a bicycle saddle. I now look at mountains more in trepidation than admiration and understand for the first time the curious punctuation in the Psalm which goes "I will lift up mine eyes unto the hills;" followed immediately by the cry "From whence cometh my help?"

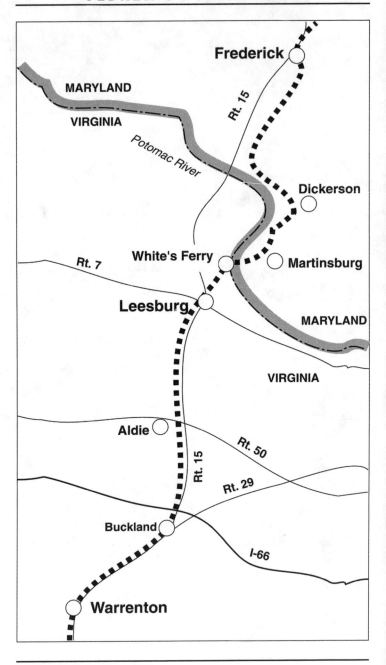

DAY 3
WARRENTON TO FREDERICK, MARYLAND

W E ARE IN MARYLAND! Yesterday we set out from Warrenton determined to double up and gain time. We weighed the benefits and liabilities and decided to risk ourselves on the shoulder of Rts. 15 & 29 north to Buckland where Rt. 15 turns off and follows the path of the Old Carolina Road towards Leesburg. We'll miss the treat of straining up and down Bust Head Road and going over Old Mother Leatherneck Mountain ... but not that much. It's not that I don't relish the opportunity to master those hills but friends in Warrenton have warned me that those particular roads are gravelled rather than paved and I tell myself that it would be better to spare the bikes.

Half an hour after our early start we have another blowout. I have to ask myself again: what is it about Mile Four? We used an expression when I was a child: 'First time accident; second time coincidence; third time enemy action.' I really am stumped on this one.

At $15 a pop these old-fashioned tubular tires are getting to be an expensive luxury. I'm now traveling without a spare. Can we get to Leesburg and a find new supply?

There's really no choice. We change tires, leave the punctured relic hanging from a road sign, and push on.

The choice of routes is good — but scary. Frank rides ahead of me so I can keep a watchful eye on him and I try to position myself a little further out on the road to make passing cars give us both a wide berth. This is a divided highway but even at 7 a.m. the 18 wheelers are gusting past at 60 miles per hour and the backdraft can be a little unnerving. I'm grateful for the heavy load on my bike. But I'm more grateful for the courtesy of the professional drivers who move over into the passing lane to give us a wide berth, sometimes downshifting and slowing until they can give us a safe margin before passing. I feel a little like a new gosling being sheltered and tolerated by the adult geese. Happily, we are off the main truck route after the first hour and the road is clear and smooth and gentle.

We're in Leesburg by 11:30, riding along the foot of the Catoctin Mountains, through Prince William with its new subdivisions, into Loudoun with its expensively-fenced horse farms, past President James Monroe's home: Oak Hill, across Goose Creek and past the National Historic Trust's Oatlands Plantation and the one-room Mountain Gap School which operated right into the 1950s right across the road.

We've made good time with only a brief halt by an Indian burial mound along the roadside. It isn't marked by any historic marker but the early Quaker settlers in nearby Lincoln recounted that right up until about 1820 a single old Indian man came each summer and performed memorial ceremonies here: the last survivor of a tribe of Piscataways whose women and children had been slaughtered by marauding Iroquois while the men were off on a hunting party. The victims were buried in this mass grave, the dwindling band of men returning each year until, for more than a decade the rituals were conducted by the last man. Then he too came no more. The mound on the side of the old north-south Carolina Road remains untouched — visited now only by those who know its story.

Leesburg is aswarm with cyclists. Not only has the town population doubled since I lived here 20 years ago but the Washington & Old Dominion Railroad right-of-way has become a bike path that stretches all the way from the Potomac River at Alexandria to the Blue Ridge Mountains at Snickers Gap: a regional park for walkers and cyclists that is about 30 yards wide and maybe 60 miles long. It's a magnet for bicyclists from all over.

The local bicycle outfitters here drop their work to help with my bike and we spend the next three hours refitting. The verdict is in on my old narrow tubular tires: they weren't designed for this kind of heavy touring and they aren't practical. They install brand new wheels that take standard clincher tires, replace the worn free-wheel sprocket at the rear whose teeth were worn down by the old chain, and tune up the brakes and derailleur gear shifter. It feels like a different bike. The new tires are almost twice the width of the old and I feel like I'm cruising in an armchair rather than rocking along on wooden rims.

We head north in the mid-afternoon, stopping briefly at the courthouse to watch a young couple being married in front of the Clerk's Office, a single delicate arch of lattice work temporarily transforming the brick and white columned courtyard into their own private wedding chapel.

We turn east a mile past Big Spring and head for White's Ferry — but not before we've cycled two miles beyond and crossed Limekiln Creek. I know this has to be wrong so we double back. No doubt some young local would be tickled pink to know that by removing the road signs he has caused us to miss the turn but it has always been one of the hazards of travel. We learn another of cycling's lessons: always note the location of landmarks like creeks, streams, power lines and even mountains that relate to the roads marked on the maps.

The Army of Northern Virginia passed this way 130 years ago although they didn't use the car ferry which now proudly advertises itself as the "Gen'l Jubal A. Early." This is the last remaining captive ferry on the Potomac that still carries cars, trucks, pedestrians and cyclists on a daily basis from 6 a.m. to 11 p.m.

I figure the ferrymam must be full of interesting tales but he's hot and angry, yelling abusively at drivers who misunderstand or ignore his instructions to arrange their cars so he can balance his small ferry. He wears a pith helmet with solar-powered fan that blows air down on his face but his nose is sunburnt bright red and he shows no interest in talking as he moves briskly from car to car collecting the fare.

We're across the river and into Maryland in less than five minutes. The Virginia cars pull off and a waiting line of Maryland cars comes aboard for the return trip. The ferryman resumes his yelling and the ferry puts back out toward the other shore. When we try to fill our water bottles at the little store run by the ferry operators they offer only bottled water at 69¢ a pint. I'm shocked until they explain that since the flood in May (which put the Potomac up six feet inside their store) their well still hasn't passed health department inspection. We study the muddy Potomac for a few minutes, wait for the traffic to clear, remount our bikes and head north for Frederick.

Locals advise us to skip the rough-graveled C & O Canal towpath which runs on the north side of the river so we take the Martinsburg and Dickerson Roads before hitting the New Design Road which runs almost ruler-straight for about eight miles into Frederick. The treat is not the anticipated straight road but up above the canal, a little section of the Martinsburg Road which appears to be a surviving section of Maryland's first paved highway system: a 10-foot-wide single lane concrete highway with four-foot wide gravelled shoulders on either side. You would almost expect to see a Model T come 'round the corner but it didn't; there wasn't any traffic at all.

Coming into Frederick we turned onto Market Street and found ourselves at the entrance to the Mount Olivet Cemetery where an impressive bronze statue marks the burial place of Francis Scott Key. He didn't die here and wasn't buried here but, his inscription explains, he was born here and years after his death the local city fathers had his remains removed from Baltimore and reburied here so they could properly honor the native son who gave us the National Anthem. His bronze effigy stands atop a granite base, his arm outstretched to a nearby flagpole where Old Glory snaps in the breeze ... "O say, can you see ..."

Through old Frederick looking for a place to put up for the night and as we got to the north end of town and prepared to go down onto Rt. 15 to a little motel a mile north we confronted a sign saying pedestrians and cyclists were prohibited. Prohibited? What were we to do?

A helpful couple out for an evening stroll gave us directions back across town to a Holiday Inn and we arrived just at dark only to find they were full. No room at the Inn? Not a one. When the Innkeeper kindly called neighboring hotels they were all likewise booked up. Any suggestions?

There was a state police barracks across the road and she suggested we might check there for ideas. Excellent! I tell Frank I've always wanted to be able to say I spent some time in jail and this would be a great part of our adventure. (It's important to keep a positive outlook even when you're exhausted.)

No luck. Sorry. The desk sergeant said they didn't let people spend the night in the cells. Not even when I offered to commit the mild misdemeanor of his choice would he relent.

A dispatcher offered to call one of the local churches that provided aid to stranded travellers and began to look through stacks of paper looking for the apparently seldom-used list.

"We're Episcopalians," I volunteered, "but Lutheran is all right. Presbyterian is fine too. Don't mind Baptist, Assembly of God, Church of the Brethren or Old Order Amish. We can even manage a few words in Latin if you've got some Roman Catholics."

While the dispatcher continued her search, the desk sergeant asked where we were headed and when I explained the problem with the sign he said we shouldn't have paid it any attention. "Oh, the sign's there all right but it's not really serious. The limited access part of the highway ends

at that intersection." He then called the motel we had originally headed for and sure enough they had a room. It was
the last one. Yes, they would hold it for us as the request of
the State Police. So we had a room, except it was across
Frederick and it was after dark.

No problem. Trooper Stanley patiently outlined a new
route for us that took us through a series of connecting
subdivisions until it put us back on Rt. 15 right at the "not
really serious" sign where we had been turned back two
hours earlier. Off we set with our headlamps waving their
little pale beams ahead and my flashing red strobe light
flickering behind us like an angry firefly.

The directions were excellent, the traffic almost non-
existent and we got in to Beckley's Motel at 10:15 p.m. It
was about 13 hours and 78 miles since we left Warrenton
and a soft bed and hot shower were rewards beyond price.
Truth is, we were ready to sleep standing up if we had to.

"Tell me something," said Mike Beckley as he handed
us the room key, "has mental illness always run in your
family?"

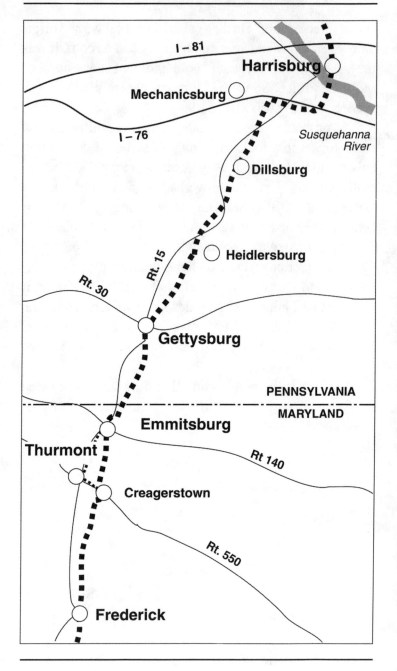

DAY 4
FREDERICK TO HARRISBURG, PENNSYLVANIA

W E ARE IN PENNSYLVANIA! Out onto Route 15 north of Frederick at dawn and pedaled up to Hansonville for a breakfast at a roadside cafe that opens at 6:30. Scrambled eggs, sausage, home fries, double toast, bottomless cup of coffee. My appetite is strong and I tuck into the food like a healthy teenager. So does my teenager. The restaurant was decorated with photos, album covers, posters and even a velvet oil painting of Elvis in all his glory and it quickly filled up with local family groups.

I asked the young waitress about the location of an old covered bridge that I'd heard is nearby on the Old Frederick Road. She'd never heard of it but knows there is one about eight or ten miles away that might be worth a side trip. We decide against it. Much as we want to take in the sights we can't afford the detour if we're to get ahead today.

We mount our bikes and half a mile north pull off the new Rt. 15 with its divided highway, fast traffic and smooth paved shoulders onto the Old Frederick Road. It's the old road across field and pasture, with old farmhouses and barns at intervals of about half a mile or so. The drought doesn't seem to have been so harsh up here and the fields look like they're supporting working farmers rather than commuting gents.

Less than a mile further, at our first creek, we see the covered bridge over Utica Creek 50 yards away: the familiar red barn siding with gable roof, covering massive old wooden beams and a heavy wooden plank flooring across a small stream 15 feet below.

This is a bridge built by craftsmen when public works were made to last and inside the covered bridge a plaque marks it as listed by the Theodore Burr Covered Bridge Society of Lancaster, Pennsylvania honoring the man who developed the Burr Arch Construction method in the last century. Another sign marks it as having been inspected by a member of the Southern Ohio Bridge Society. Yet another reminds us that "Willful damage or destruction of a covered bridge is a crime punishable by law." I should think so.

It seems to be well-known at least to bicyclists and two separate groups pass through as we walk around admiring its construction.

We pedal on after our brief rest, bound for Emmitsburg and Gettysburg, following the path of the Army of Northern Virginia.

In late June of 1863 they marched north seeking a decisive victory that would break the north's resolve to continue the war. A week later they struggled south with a wagon train more than 18 miles long filled with their wounded and dying. The countryside looks unchanged: still dotted with barns, farmhouses, pens and outbuildings; still crisscrossed with fence rows; still looking rich and appealing.

One thing that has definitely not changed is the timeless humor of rotating the signposts at the crossroads. We discover the joke when we come into Thurmont instead of Emmitsburg. So it's back onto the new Rt. 15 with its heavy traffic but mercifully wide paved shoulders and make yet another mental note to always check landmarks before believing signposts.

We pass a large sign erected by the citizens and Governor of Maryland thanking us for visiting, asking us to come again. Two hundred yards on is another large sign: this one put up by the Governor of Pennsylvania welcoming us to his state. We take it personally. It's nice to be thanked for visiting. It's pleasant to be welcomed. Thank you. The pleasure is ours. Really.

Soon we're back on the old road. We leave the traffic behind. The Catoctin Mountains stretch north on our left. The gentle rolling farmland falls away to our right.

Bicycling is a process of continuing physical exertion and forced introspection. You hear the birds sing, the cars or trucks rush by, the breeze ripple through the corn and wheatfields. Your thoughts are your own and sometimes they play tricks on you.

Mine say "Hurry up. Hurry up." I imagine a corps commander urging his troops to close up ranks. "Push on. Close up. Close up."

I want to say "We're coming. We're coming" but I know we're too late. 130 years too late. I realize we're at the edge of America's bloodiest battlefield when the first artillery piece looms up in a small clearing on our right with an historic marker explaining the early position of Union troops.

We pedal on. Up hill and down. Then we're out of the woods. Into the open.

The Gettysburg Battlefield unfolds north of us with a suddenness that takes my breath away. A rocky grey outcropping in the distance across a wheat field must be Devil's Den. The green wooded hill must be Little Round Top. The observation tower, cyclorama and orchard mark the famous Angle. The fields are studded with cannon and stone monuments marking each regiment's position.

This road has been kept virtually unchanged since the battle — since Pickett's Charge — since that awful July 3rd, 1863 when the Confederate troops came out of Spangler's Woods, walked almost a mile across open fields exploding with cannon and musket shot, performed their 45 degree oblique turn, halted to dress right, reformed their line of battle and then broke into a sort of jog that carried them up to the Union lines where the exhausted, shell-shocked, wounded and shattered remnants finally broke the Union line only to find there weren't enough men left to hold their ground and no reserves to follow up their charge.

"We gained nothing but glory," said one survivor, "and lost our bravest men."

No one can visit Gettysburg without being profoundly moved by the bravery and valor of men on both sides. Having come up that hot dry road in the searing heat of a hot summer morning, dripping sweat, I have a physical sense of their exertions. Surely it was the Valley of the Shadow of Death made manifest for them all.

Across that Emmitsburg Road my son's great-great grand uncle, Lewis Burwell Williams, too ill to advance on foot, rode on horseback to lead his men in the First Virginia Regiment of Kemper's Brigade and knowingly became a prime target for the Union sharpshooters on the hillside.

He was the first officer to be killed in Pickett's charge.

We continue up the road and turn in to view the cyclorama, to see the original pencilled draft of Lincoln's Gettysburg address, to study the diagrams of this awful struggle, to walk among the hushed tourists who look at the small stone which marks the spot in the Angle where Confederate General Lewis Armistead fell mortally wounded, leading his troops against those commanded by his devoted friend, the Union General William Hancock. Stone after stone marks the position of the Union defenders. Park Rangers lead tour after tour and people of all ages wander the ridge to ponder the meaning of this national crucible of fire and steel and blood and death where 50,000 Americans were reported killed, wounded, captured or missing.

After almost an hour of walking the ridge and pointing out the positions of the different regiments I ask my son Frank if I have stuffed enough history down his throat for one day. "Oh, you can keep on if you want," he answers drolly. "I haven't been paying any attention."

We take our lunch at Hardee's, across the road from the Cyclorama and I'm relieved that national marketing has superimposed "Frisco Burgers" on the menu rather than "Meade-burgers" or "Lee-fries", "Yankee-dogs" or "Rebel-Chicken." For some reason I myself don't have much appetite after all this history. A cold drink in the shade is a powerful restorative.

We originally planned to spend the night at the Gettysburg Youth Hostel, just down the street from where Lincoln gave his famous speech, but we have gained time and distance and determine to push on to Harrisburg. We put our bikes back on the old road headed north, crossing and recrossing the new road with its big trucks and speeding traffic. At the top of one long steady rising hill, at a place our map calls Clear Spring, we halt and pitch our bikes against the road bank, happy to collapse for a moment, drain a water bottle, lie on our backs and look at the clouds.

A voice calls out from across the road "Hey! Over here!" and a 60-something retiree waves vigorously at us. I dread the thought of being told to move along by some irate local but no, he is beckoning us.

"Over here," he repeats. "Got a water spigot behind the bush. Use the table and benches in the shade."

John Hoffman is what you might call a cycle-groupie. His house, he explains, is about halfway between Carlisle and Frederick and he has made his yard a regular watering hole for the area bicycle clubs. He not only gives us fresh cool water but goes over our maps and details the local landmarks to look for, advice on hills, new construction, missing street signs — "Look for the Korean Church sign instead..."

I think he would have mounted his own bike and led us to Harrisburg but he and his wife were already late to a meeting. He waved us on with great reluctance.

We pedal on. Some really sweet downhill coasting. Some really draining uphill climbs. Some tiresome walks. We turn off the Old Gettysburg Road onto Winding Hill

Road and I see it is aptly named: the hills stretch out ahead of us, higher and higher. More and more up. Less and less down. It's daunting.

Straining up a small rise I feel the gear lever wiggle and then swing loose in my hand. The cable has parted. Disaster. I now have only top gear. Fine for downhill. All right for level. Impossible for uphill.

We are still six miles from our destination and have only about a half hour of daylight left. Distant farmhouses and rolling fields offer little hope of repairs. Nothing for it but push on. One slow steady revolution of the pedals after another.

Push. Strain. One more turn. Don't look up. Concentrate on the pavement directly in front of the wheel. Sweat runs off me in a steady stream. I try not to wobble off the road. This has become an endurance test. It has become the Bataan Death March.

A car pulls up behind us, slows, honks noisily, then swishes past. It's one of the new small vans. The driver is shaking his fist out the window and yells something unintelligible. He pulls over and stops. Jumps out. I get ready for a rude altercation and slow my bike to a halt.

Praise God! It's Larry Jones, my classmate at school in England 25 years ago, who is now a minister in Harrisburg. His house is our destination for the evening. Being a Presbyterian, he naturally believes in pre-destination, and, we being late in arriving, he has set out with his small daughters to see if he can find us *pre*-destination. He has.

Hallelujah!

Bikes into the van in minutes and then he carries us the last three miles — the last three hilly miles — to our destination. There's nothing like a taste of salvation to give one religion.

Larry, his wife Cindy, and daughters Campbell and Frances make us feel right at home and well we should. They live on Peyton Randolph Place in a neighborhood whose street names all appear to have been culled from a directory of Colonial Williamsburg residents. (The long reach of the Old Dominion stretches out across the land).

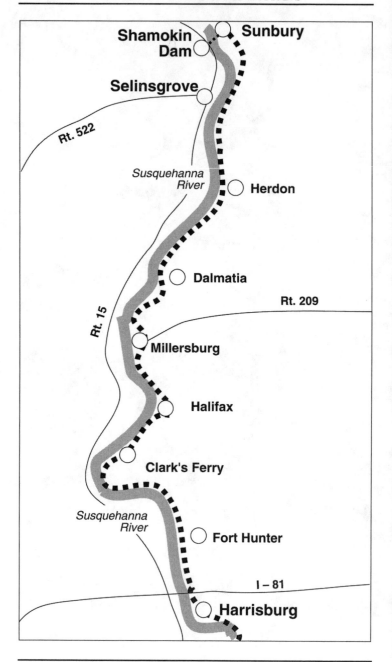

DAY 5
HARRISBURG TO SHAMOKIN DAM

W E ARE ON THE BANKS of the Susquehanna River at Shamokin Dam! (I always thought Jay Unger and Molly Mason were playing a tune called Shamokin Good-bye but my wife insists their haunting melody is actually called 'Ashoken Farewell').

Shamokin Dam on the other hand is famous for the "the largest inflatable fabridam in the world" a dam which backs up a lake of 3,000 acres on the Susquehanna.

Yesterday we covered 61 miles in 7 hours, heavy going but not nearly as bad as trying to do it without gears. In the morning Larry Jones showed us an almost entirely downhill route from his house to a local bicycle shop and when we arrived they immediately dropped their work to get us going again. Bicycle shop mechanics always seem to have more work than they can handle but every one of them is willing to drop everything to get long distance tourers back on the road.

Owner Scott Stewart's young assistant referred to my bike as a "dinosaur" but Scott was more diplomatic: "You know," he said, as he studied my bike, "this is a real 're-storable'. People are collecting old bikes like this with original equipment and restoring them. Some of them are worth big money." A 'restorable'? Heavens. The bike isn't even half as old as I am.

Lucky for me Scott has a box of 'obsolete' parts that came with the store when he bought it. He not only has a cable that will fit, he also has a "new" derailleur gearshifter to replace mine which has been bent under the strain. "This is at least 15 years old," he says proudly. "You won't see another one like it on the roads today."

Replacing the derailleur leads him to check the spokes and he demonstrates how spongy they've become. "I'd be scared to think what might happen if you're coming down a hill with all this weight behind you and the wheel fell apart," he says. So it's off with the wheel, tighten the spokes one by one, true up the hub and then reassemble again.

I'm grateful for small mercies. In this case, I'm grateful for large mercies too. When we set off at noon the bike feels solid again. The gears switch back and forth almost effortlessly. It feels like a new machine and I realize somewhat ruefully that if we continue to replace worn parts at this rate, my valuable 'restorable' may be entirely new by the time we reach Canada.

We cross into Harrisburg on the Walnut Street Bridge — one of those old steel truss spans with steel grating for a surface that lets you look down at the mighty river 60-feet below you as you pedal slowly across. (This is the river that widens to form the Chesapeake Bay but don't expect your friends on the Potomac, Rappahannock, York or James Rivers to believe you.)

Along Front Street and then up Rt. 147 on the east side of the Susquehanna. It's a gentle uphill grade that parallels the old canal towpath. A light drizzle falls steadily during the afternoon but we pedal on through it. We expect to be wet when we're cycling and this is a welcome change from the searing heat of the sun.

We stop for a late lunch in Millersburg where the local lunch counter serves excellent old-fashioned, thick, lumpy, milk shakes. The talk all revolves around the incredible accident last night in Harrisburg. A local woman witnessed a head-on collision which resulted in one car bursting into flame. She helped pull the unrecognizable driver from the wreck and began to administer CPR but couldn't save him despite 20 minutes of intense effort. Only when the ambulance crew took over and she could see the tattoos on his chest did she realize the victim was her own younger brother. We finish our meal in silence and move on.

North of Millersburg the road is lined with ancient Sycamore trees, making it look almost like stretches of the Loire Valley in France. The river flows quietly on the left, the traffic is light, the grade is only a modest uphill and the heavily wooded mountains rise high on either side. I have come to love river valleys. I have developed a dislike for mountains that borders on irrational passion. They're nice to look at, welcome companions alongside, but when they're across my path they're beasts of another kind.

I still walk up the steepest hills. Even with the new gear cable and tune up there's no question of being prideful. "Pride goeth before destruction and an haughty spirit before a fall" says the Proverb — I don't need either.

The lesson of Frederick fresh in my mind, and daylight dimming with the mountains on both sides of us, I stop at a local store and enquire about motels. There aren't any on this side of the river but there's a Comfort Inn across the river about eight miles up. We call ahead and make a reservation. Damp and fatigue are powerful arguments for a hot shower and a clean bed.

We cross the Susquehanna at Shamokin Dam and head for the Comfort Inn on Rt. 15. I spy the sign from the bridge and pick up my speed. I dismount at the curbside and walk my bike across the lawn, declining to pedal an extra 50 yards to their entrance and the formal curved driveway up to the office.

"I guess someone must be anxious to check in," says Frank in a loud stage whisper to no one in particular.

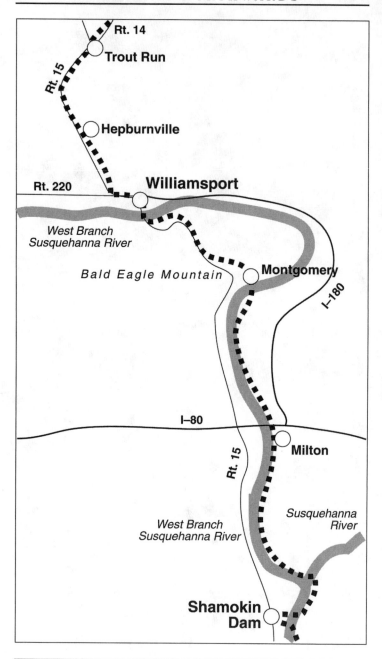

DAY 6
SHAMOKIN DAM TO TROUT RUN

W E ARE IN TROUT RUN, PENNSYLVANIA! — in the mountains about 14 miles north of Williamsport — more than halfway to Canada! We have spent the night at the Hemlock Motel — a roadside stop where my family used to overnight every year going to and coming from Virginia. Towering hemlocks still crowd up to the back of the motel crouched at the foot of the mountain but time has wrought its changes. The road was re-engineered and the grade raised considerably back in the early 60s when the highway was widened and speeds increased. The dining room has been discontinued and the "new" swimming pool (which was built in the late 60s to lure the dwindling traffic) is permanently closed.

The line of rooms with doors facing onto the gravelled parking lot are as I remember them, but smaller. The clusters of guests, sitting outside their rooms, watching the evening light grow dim, are vanished. The parking lot has two cars rather than 20.

I recall chasing my brothers and sisters around the crowded parking lot and over to the picnic tables — a treat for us children after endless hours cooped up in a hot car. I remember long walks in the evening to inspect an arrowhead collection at a neighboring farmer's would-be tourist attraction. Memories of bow and arrow practice at the edge of the woods flit back into my mind's eye and pull along with them the fear that came at dark: fear that near-naked Iroquois might be lurking in the higher shadows with knives and tomahawks, sneaking up to kill and scalp the grown-ups, carry the children off into captivity. We were wildly impressionable children when television was in its infancy and James Fennimore Cooper was still common bedtime reading.

This landmark is a inheritance of my childhood, full of repeated associations. Now I have passed it on my son. Whether it survives for his children depends on so many things. When I look at the trends I have my doubts.

Yesterday we covered 48 miles of surprisingly gentle upgrades all along the east side of the Susquehanna up to Montgomery where we crossed the river again and stopped for lunch at Leone's Original Italian Pizza Restaurant.

Leone's was recommended by two teenage entrepreneurs who were out delivering the local shopper and came over to welcome us to their town when we stopped to take our bearings at the curbside. Leone is one of their customers and they happily joined us with a proprietary air, placing us at a front table to look out on the almost deserted main street.

Leone himself turns out to be Yugoslavian — not Italian — and he moved here from Richlands, Virginia. He wishes he were back again. "People much friendlier," he says. "Much more open. Better business." He mourns the destruction of his homeland and grieves for friends and relatives. Milosevic, he says, is an evil man. Leone is grateful to be in America.

At the suggestion of the young entrepreneurs, we abandon our route along the east side of the Susquehanna in favor of a shortcut over Rt. 54 to Rt. 15 at the foot of Bald Eagle Mountain. It will cut seven miles off our trip. I look at the mountain contours on the map and calculate the trade-off is worth it. When we actually come up against the mountain I have second thoughts. No sign of any bald eagles but plenty of the beastly mountain.

Frank peddles ahead to await me on the summit. I dismount and walk as the grade quickly overpowers me. It's a steady steep push and the bike seems to weigh more than before. Even walking up along the paved shoulder becomes a strain. I begin to hallucinate. A flatbed truck downshifts as it passes me carrying a Caterpillar tractor and I realize it is going slow enough for me to almost keep up with it. Maybe I should exert myself and pass it. Imagine the surprise on the driver's face if I passed by pushing my bike. Fat chance.

Dripping with sweat and my chest heaving to draw in fresh breath I finally reach the top. Frank is already rested up and ready to go. It has been only three miles but taken me more than an hour. Now we can go on. Go down. Coast. Enjoy the breeze. Oh yes, a breezy downhill coast: I love it.

We stopped at the scenic overlook above Williamsport and tried to take in the magnificence of the view across to Allegheny Ridge 12 or 15 miles away. The view is wider than your field of vision. You have to turn your head to take it all in. Far down in the distance you can see small planes taking off from an airport. We are almost a half mile above the river and have an unobstructed view from east-north-east all the way to west. And we got here under our own steam.

When I was a child cars and trucks all used to line up along this section of roadside but not for the scenic overlook. Then it was for the little spring coming out of the rock where motorists could refill their overheated radiators and wait for their cars to cool down after the hard pull up the mountain.

We rest our weary legs and then it is down and down, brakes constantly applied trying to keep the bikes under control and under 40 miles per hour. Scary, yes, but oh what a treat.

Into South Williamsport past the National Little League Hall of Fame and slowed for the approach to the Susquehanna Bridge. A metallic clatter sounded as I ran over a piece of broken tailpipe and a sudden squishy-ness under me announced another rear tire blowout. I'm grateful it hadn't happened at high speed but not to worry. This is the first puncture since Warrenton and we're now experienced hands at tire changing. Not quite as fast as the 20-second changeovers of the Tour duPont riders but 25 minutes isn't bad for us heavy cavalry types. The best part is that I only have to replace the inner tube with a spare and I can patch the punctured inner tube later when we stop for the night: giving me a serviceable spare again.

Through downtown Williamsport about 4 o'clock and decided to push on to Trout Run — another two hours beyond. A fairly moderate upgrade with tall forested mountains on all sides. This is the section of Pennsylvania that I have dreaded. Mountain after mountain that seem to stretch on into Canada. It's a grand place to study upthrusts, faulting, and erosion but it loses much of its scientific appeal if you have to pedal your way over every single one of these geologic specimens.

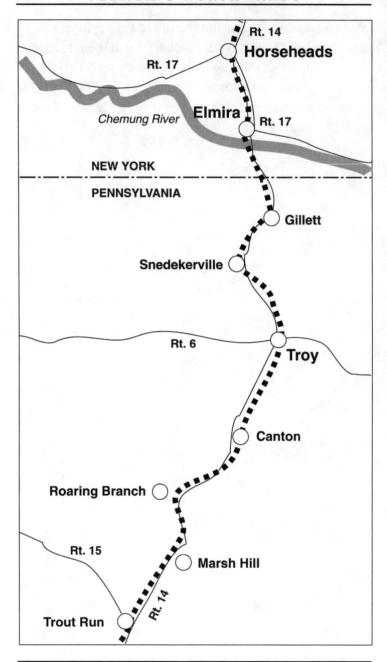

DAY 7
TROUT RUN TO HORSEHEADS

W e're in New York State! Yesterday we covered 67 miles through the mountains of Pennsylvania and discovered to our amazement that you can indeed go through the mountains without going over them. It's true. I feel like we've threaded the needle but it's another argument in favor of the experienced cyclist's advice to seek out the river valleys and avoid new roads.

We left Trout Run in the morning after a leisurely breakfast of pancakes and sausage and coffee that kept on coming, at the Steam Valley Restaurant. When I tried to buy a postcard as we left, the waitress hurried over to the counter to say with some embarrassment "Oh, there's no charge. When I told the cook where you'd come from and where you're headed he asked what I had given you for the trip. I told him I had only just found you were bicycling to Canada and he said we had to give you something for luck. So the post card is free. Have a safe ride!"

What a send-off. I believe I am more strengthened by the sentiments than by the sausage and pancakes.

We part company today with the heavily-travelled Rt. 15 and decide to follow old Rt. 14, the pre-revolutionary war road along the Lycoming River Valley that was the original Sheshequin Path — "the Great Road" of the Iroquois Indians.

To my amazement, shortly after we set out we come upon an Historic Marker that notes we are not the first to come this way from the Old Dominion: "By this path up Lycoming Creek," it says, "Conrad Weiser, with Lewis Evans map-maker, and John Bartram, botanist, traveled to Onondaga in 1743 on a peace mission for Virginia: 'To take the hatchet out of the hand of the Six Nations.'"

Exactly 250 years ago to the week, Pennsylvania's famed Indian Agent Conrad Weiser led an expedition on behalf of our own Lt. Governor William Gooch of Virginia to appease the Iroquois after a skirmish between an Indian hunting party and settlers in western Virginia. "If possible," wrote Governor Gooch, "prevail with them to accept through Your Hands a Present from Us of £100 Sterl value in such Goods as you think proper as a token of our sincere Disposition to preserve Peace and friendship with them…"

Evans later marked the Alleghennies here as 'The Endless Mountains' and the Lycoming Valley as a 'dismal wilderness' in his 1753 map; describing their arrival in Shamokin he wrote in his journal "Descending the hill, it was so steep, we were obliged to hold the horse which carried our baggage, both by the head and tail, to prevent his tumbling headlong."

When they finally arrived in Onondaga, the Iroquois capital which is the site of present-day Syracuse, Weiser himself told the Iroquois chieftain Tocanontie "It was enough to kill a Man to come such a Long and bad Road over Hills, Rocks, Old Trees and Rivers, and to fight through a Cloud of Vermine, and all kinds of Poison'd Worms and creeping things ..."

I sympathize extremely but am forced to admit that the road has improved a little over the intervening years.

Old roads along river valleys are level. They're almost always flat. There's none of this modern dynamite engineering that carries superhighways straight up a mountain side without regard for the stamina of ox, horse, mule or man. This Sheshequin Path was obviously chosen by people who had looked at the alternatives in this range of 'endless mountains.'

We have encountered our first serious headwinds this morning. At first I thought it was a pleasant cooling breeze but when I found myself struggling to maintain 10 m.p.h. on a downhill grade I realized we had run into some stiff opposition. Level is good. Cool is good. Smooth is good. Tailwinds are good. Headwinds? We hates 'em. They might just as well be mountains.

Stopped for lunch in Troy where Frank discovered the joys of a flavored soda.

"What's a flavored soda," he asked the waitress after he looked at her menu. "I thought sodas were already flavored."

"Well, she replied, "it's a Coke or a Pepsi or Sprite with flavoring added: cherry, lemon-lime, orange or chocolate ... You'll like it."

"Okay. Chocolate coke."

"Good choice," she said.

And moments later he was savoring the Troy Lunch's flavored soda. "Good choice," he agreed. It's the sort of small town originality and creativity that you can't get if you don't have any old-fashioned soda fountain or the willingness to experiment and improve on what the national marketing gurus think is classic perfection — uh-hunh.

Crossed into New York State and the road immediately changed its name to Broadway. (You've really got to give credit to these New Yorkers when it comes to marketing). Governor Mario Cuomo has put up a sign here welcoming us to his state and we are as charmed as we were entering Maryland and Pennsylvania. It's reassuring to be on a personal basis with so many top officials.

Pedaled north to Elmira and straight onto Walnut Street past the Woodlawn Cemetery whose chief attraction is being the final resting place of Mark Twain.

Mark Twain? The southern humorist? The Mississippi's Mark Twain? Samuel Clemens?

I half expected to see a family plot with tombstones for all his literary children: Tom and Huck and Injun Joe and maybe Pudd'nhead Wilson but no... they are immortal and shall never be buried. The adjoining tombstones are for Mark Twain's wife (a native of Elmira) and his real children, including one for a young daughter that bears the inscription "This stone placed by her desolate father."

The family marker has likenesses of both Twain and his son-in-law, Ossip Gabrilowitsch who asked to be buried at Twain's feet. The tall stone column is exactly 12 feet high — two fathoms — mark twain — the minimum depth for a riverboat.

Further up the road is Elmira's National Cemetery where almost 3,000 Confederate prisoners of war are buried in rank after rank beneath small white numbered headstones giving their name, regiment and state. In the winter of 1864-65, one out of four southern prisoners died in the bitterly cold northern winter. All of the states of the Confederacy are represented in this distant field: Alabama, Arkansas, Florida, Georgia, Kentucky, Louisiana, Mississippi, South Carolina, Virginia and North Carolina.

So many from North Carolina. It seems almost four of five: the reluctant secessionist, last to leave the Union, the state that suffered the largest number of casualties of all ...

A few stones are marked only with a number and the inscription "Unknown, CSA"

One stands a little taller than the others, a darker stone: it marks the grave of John Smitht, aged 34 years "This stone placed by his oldest son, John Smitht, now living in Opelika, Kansas."

Lest we forget.

Our nation's history is preserved in our graveyards. Mark Twain was not just southern or western or southwestern. Tom Sawyer and Huckleberry Finn belong to America. So does Mark Twain. Those southern patriots who lie buried in their ranks at the Elmira National Cemetery belong to America too.

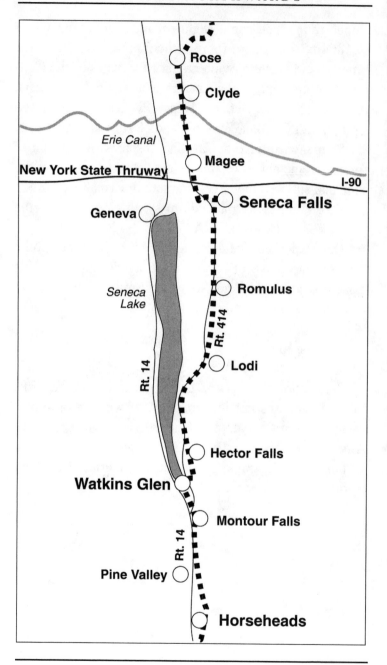

DAY 8
HORSEHEADS TO ROSE RIDGE

W E'RE WITHIN FIVE MILES OF LAKE ONTARIO! Yes terday we covered 84 miles, putting us 537 miles from Richmond. And — joy of joys — we have discovered that north of Elmira, New York the rivers flow north instead of south. We have crossed over the divide and our path is now technically downhill.

(So much for the advice of starting in Canada and coasting downhill to Virginia.)

Rt. 14 north of Elmira follows Catherine Creek which empties into Seneca Lake at Watkins Glen and it's a bona fide downhill grade where we averaged more than 15 miles an hour — our best yet. Frank and I are both anxious to see Lake Ontario, to gaze across the lake at Canada and so we skip the racing car museum and push on up the east side of the lake, up onto the ridge that gives us a constant view down on those turquoise waters for the next 30 miles.

We halt for lunch at the Ginny Lee Cafe — an elegant restaurant with linen tablecloths, shiny silverware and sparkling wine glasses, run by the owners of the surrounding Wagner Vineyard. The sight of the outside deck with its tables and chairs encourages us to risk our sweaty, earthy appearance in a public place. The deck sweeps around the huge barn-like building offering diners a view over the neat rows of grape vines to Seneca Lake which is constantly changing color as cloud shadows race across the deep blue-green waters. It's a perfect afternoon with bright and sun and stiff breeze. Perfect, that is, for sitting on a deck and eating bread and cheese and sampling the Wagner's featured Gewurztraminer.

Oh Glory! Oh civilization! Indeed, this is not the Bataan Death March!

An hour later, feeling thoroughly rejuvenated, we remount our bikes and push into the strong headwinds that have so artistically rushed the fluffy clouds over the lake. I immediately regret the lapse of discipline that led me to indulge myself in that superb New York wine and brought on a state of relaxation that isn't at all prepared for the necessary push. Isn't it the Book of Proverbs that warns of wine "At the last it biteth like a serpent and stingeth like an adder ...?"

We arrived in Seneca Falls about 4 o'clock and found ourselves in front of the National Women's Hall of Fame on Fall Street before we even had a chance to ask directions. Here, in 1848, at the Wesleyan Methodist Chapel, the first convention for Women's Rights was held and the Declaration of Sentiments issued.

It was a radical declaration which called for reform in divorce, property, labor, electoral, and even church laws, insisting on "immediate admission to all the rights and privileges which belong to [women] as citizens of the United States." Seventy-two years later the 19th Amendment granted women the right to vote. A hundred and forty-five years later, as we watch the Wesleyan Chapel undergoing restoration for a new National Park Center, the Women's Rights struggle still goes on.

Against a small sycamore tree we find two other touring bicycles with more gear on them than our own and we meet Steve Anastasia and Christy Denzl who set off this summer from Lowell, Massachusetts on their way to Colorado. They hope to get to Arizona before the big snows. Our trip to Canada pales by comparison. We exchange notes on the road and wish each other luck. Misery loves company and it's always encouraging to know there are at least a few other people with the same eccentricities.

From Seneca Falls we push north again on 414. Flat farming countryside. Amish country. The shoulders are paved and wide enough for the Amish horse-drawn buggies — ideal for cycling. Even the occasional road apples — a more common form of pollution in the days before automobiles — pose no hazard to our passage. But we are both struck by the incongruity of the highway department's fresh white line painted right overtop of the recent horse-droppings, a tree limb, a long-dead groundhog and a recently-killed squirrel.. We've seen a lot of roadkill on our trip: deer, groundhog, possum, rabbit, dog, cats and mice but this is the first place we've seen them become part of the highway.

It is smooth going all the way up 414 to the little village of Rose where we turn off on a side road at the War Memorial. This tiny village must have seen better days. The simple stone marker commemorates the sacrifices of residents who have fought and died in the wars of 1776, 1812, 1846, 1861, 1898, 1917, 1941, 1950, and 1964 .. We can only pray they add no more dates in Rose.

We arrive at the Rose Ridge Youth Hostel just at dark. It's an old farm house that has been expanded by successive generations and now has abundant space for adventurous travellers. We are welcomed by a note from Manager Renée Regis telling us to feel at home and help ourselves to anything we need. She has to be out in the evening but the door is always open and more hostelers can be expected. Sure enough, we are later joined by an English lecturer who has been on an exchange at the University of West Virginia, a Californian who is travelling the east to get her head together, and an incoming graduate student at the University of Rochester who is scouting out an apartment for the fall. This hospitality to strangers is one of the most impressive discoveries of our trip.

We are impressed, and deeply grateful for a bed to sleep in.

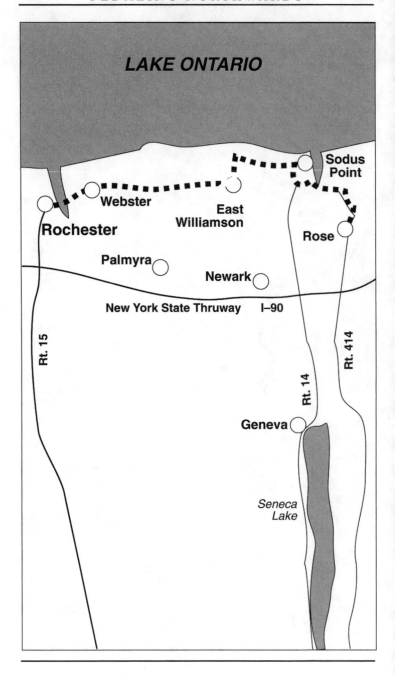

DAY 9
ROSE RIDGE TO ROCHESTER

W E ARE IN ROCHESTER — on the shore of Lake Ontario! We pedaled 64 miles yesterday and are now more than 600 miles from Richmond on the James. We breakfasted yesterday morning at the Town Café in Wolcott where the talk was all hushed amazement at the news of a local man who used his pocketknife to cut off his own leg after being pinned by a falling tree; he then crawled half a mile to get help. Some wonder whey he didn't use his pocketknife on the tree. Others wonder about his mental state.

One asks "You mean before or after?"

I try to concentrate on breakfast but we leave a little earlier than usual.

We reach the shore of Lake Ontario about 10 o'clock and pedal right down onto the sandy beach at Sodus Point, reaching our hands into the lakesurf in a symbolic gesture of accomplishment. There's a stiff breeze and the waves are running about a foot high out of the northwest.

Contrary to my expectation we can't see Canada across the lake. This is, after all, one of the Great Lakes. They say it's at least 60 miles across here. Must be. I'm ready to believe 'em.

At Frank's suggestion, we decide to check the harbor to see if there are any boats bound for Toronto; see if we can talk our way aboard, offer to work our way across. It's not that we're averse to cycling all the way but the idea of sitting on a deck chair while the wind does the work has a certain appeal after 10 days in the saddle and we think it might be equally adventurous.

Unfortunately we have no luck. Several boaters are sympathetic but they point out that most yachts are holed up in the harbor right now waiting for the wind to diminish: it's too rough for most of them to attempt a crossing. The distance to Toronto is more than 120 nautical miles — at least 12 hours in the best of winds and this isn't the best of winds. It's driving right out of Toronto at 10 to 12 knots. Better to check in the harbor at Rochester.

So it's saddle up, feet back in the stirrups and take our long-planned left turn onto the old Lakeshore Highway toward Rochester. It's a not a path we stay on long.

The wind coming off the lake is so fierce we almost have to tack back and forth on the narrow road to make progress. Just past Bootlegger's Point I call and a halt and we study our maps. Decide to move up onto the old Ridge Road — Rt. 104. We head uphill on Townline Road and I regret the decision immediately. I hate hills with a deep passion. They're as menacing as mountains.

Once we're onto Ridge Road it lives up to its name. No more up and down over every creek and stream which empties into the lake. The shoulders aren't much good but the traffic is light and we push right along.

East of Webster we stop for a cold drink and the storekeeper immediately adopts us. He also works as a paid fireman in Rochester and he takes it upon himself to get us across Irondequoit Bay and through the city without hitting any major traffic. Within minutes he has sketched out a detailed map that takes us off the main road, through subdivisions, parks and even a golf course before landing us at the Riverview Yacht Club on the Genessee River. The routing is ideal. We pass through this city of 230,000 (almost the size of Richmond) as if through a small village and arrive at the harbor just as the Spirit of Rochester puts out with its boatload of evening revellers. The Captain, standing at the gangplank taking tickets ($47 per person for all you can eat Prime Rib supper with open bar) gives us directions to some Canadian boats moored further back where we might get passage.

We pedal back and make our pitch but no luck. Even the big motor launches are holed up waiting for the wind to moderate. One skipper tells us he tried three days ago but turned back only a quarter of the way over, afraid his boat would get beaten to pieces.

Nothing for it but to find a hotel before dark and set out again in the morning. There was a Comfort Inn three miles away. I've learned my lesson about calling ahead. Yes they had a room. It was their last one. It had a Jacuzzi. A Jacuzzi? No problem.

Flat is good. Tailwinds are great. Jacuzzi should be terrific.

For those of you who, like me, don't have a Jacuzzi and have never been to a hotel with one, a Jacuzzi is like a bathtub but it's the size of a large dinghy with water inside instead of outside. Where the oarlocks ought to be they have nozzles that squirt the hot water around you like the old hospital whirlpool baths.

Luckily the whole system is on a timer that turns itself off automatically after 10 minutes. Otherwise I expect people wouldn't quit. They'd relax into a stupor, fall asleep and drown. At least I reckon they would if they'd just pedaled 64 miles across upstate New York.

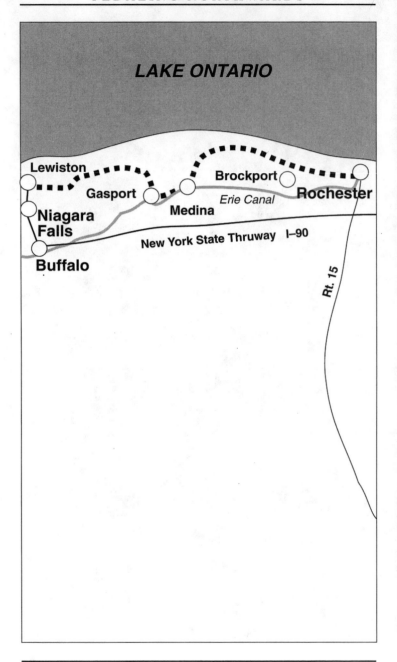

DAY 10
ROCHESTER TO NIAGARA

O CANADA! O CANADA! This, our last day riding from Virginia to Canada, has been our best yet: we covered more than 90 miles, leaving Rochester about 7:30 a.m. and crossed the international border at Lewiston almost exactly 12 hours later.

Not only did we cover the distance, we had time to stop in the morning at a coin laundromat and eat a wonderful breakfast of Breuggel's Bagels as we watched our shirts, shorts, socks and smalls tumble round and round in the dryer. Strangely satisfying to just sit still and watch something else go round and round and round.

I have pulled out ahead this morning to set the pace and about four miles out I notice Frank's absence in the little rearview mirror mounted on my left handlebar. I pull over and halt, turn about and scan the road behind me. No Frank. We have an agreement about always maintaining sight contact as a matter of safety and I have breached the rule. So it's turn about and head back. Vigorous pedaling for about a half mile and there he is on the side of the road crouching beside his front wheel.

It's a puncture: his first.

I still can't figure out what it is about the four-mile mark that leads to punctures but we're pretty good at the procedure. Changing this one only takes 15 minutes and we're off again through vineyards and orchards of apples, peaches and cherries.

We drop down off the Ridge Road to get lunch at Medina and discover the Erie Canal. It's still operational here but used now as a waterway for pleasure boats, rather than a commercial freight line trying to capture the trade coming out of the west.

We head west again after lunch but this time along the old towpath: a treat to ride on. At some points the houses come right down to the canal, looking like a village in Holland, at others the open fields stretch away to the distance on either side. Sometimes we found ourselves peddling alongside the canal with not a house or barn or structure anywhere within view.

To our great disappointment the graveled towpath began to get rougher and rather than risk a mechanical failure in the middle of the wheat fields we reluctantly came off at Millersport and headed back up to the relative safety of the Ridge Road.

I say "relative safety" because as we headed toward Lewiston the traffic began to pick up and just out of Gasport I reached for my rear brake lever on a downhill coast and found it loose in my hand. The ancient cable yoke had parted under the relentless strain. Now all I would have would be the front brakes and they couldn't hold all this weight on a steep hill. From here on it would be caution, caution and caution ... with both feet dragging on the road if necessary.

About 5:30, our water supplies almost exhausted, we began to get desperate for a cold drink and decided to pull in at the next available stop. A roadside store loomed in the distance. The first one we'd seen in about six miles: a beer joint.

Three waitresses and five customers clustered 'round the bar nursing bottled beers. I apologized for our sweaty appearance as we came in and apologized again for not ordering their fine beer; then asked for any tall cold soft drink they could provide us.

Naturally a silence descended on them as we entered but then a good-natured ribbing started about turkeys on bikes — a ribbing that stopped completely when we smilingly told them where we'd come from and where we were headed.

"Considering how far you've come," said the waitress, "I guess these drinks are on the house," and she placed two huge ice-filled glasses of Pepsi in front of us.

A 30-something construction worker looks us over and asks "If you're from Virginia, how come you sound like Canadians? Say 'out and about'."

"You mean 'out and about the house'" I answer.

"Yeah. You sound just like Canadians."

"Well," I replied. "I grew up in Canada but we have that broad 'o' in parts of Virginia too. A lot of the settlers in Ontario were United Empire Loyalists who came up from the States after the Revolutionary War. I guess some were from Virginia."

"I was stationed in Virginia," said another of our new-found friends. "Stationed at Dam Neck. You ever heard of

Dam Neck? Didn't think so. Very secure base. Handled Polaris missiles for the submarines. Very secure.

"When I got my orders for Dam Neck I went to Greyhound for a ticket and they told me weren't no such damn place on this damn earth as Dam Neck, Virginia. So I had to go back to the base and they said 'Well, you get a ticket to Virginia Beach and the Navy'll handle it from there.' Sure enough. They did. Very secure base. Marines everywhere. You couldn't get in 'less you had all your papers in order."

We thanked the waitresses and left the patrons discussing the military strategy of having secure bases in places you couldn't get to, grateful for the lifesaving drink and the generosity of strangers. We still had miles to go before we slept.

West and west along the Ridge Road right into Lewiston with the great Niagara Escarpment rising on our left. Straining up the heights we can see the skyscrapers and CN Tower of Toronto 30 miles away across the lake. We've almost made it.

In the near distance we can see a tall stone column — maybe 200 feet tall — with a bronze statue of Canada's General Brock on the top. He died at the Battle of Queenston Heights repelling an American invasion force during the War of 1812: the last serious conflict between our two nations who now boast the longest undefended border in the world. The column is on the Canadian side of the border so we must be within a mile or less.

Pushing heavily against the pedals, trying not to get off and walk, we suddenly found ourselves funneled into a spaghetti of overpasses and underpasses that put us out onto

... I didn't believe it ... we were headed onto the New York State Thruway! Impossible. Couldn't be.

Sure was.

All our efforts to avoid traffic end in this: within sight of Canada we are now peddling along an Interstate headed for the border crossing.

Up the ramp, onto the bridge. My heart is pounding and I try not to look down through the steel grating at the Niagara River pouring through its gorge 300 feet below. Keep pedaling. Keep pushing. Traffic is slowing. Cars are backing up. It's the Customs Station. We are in Canada!

About 20 cars ahead I see a Customs official, wearing a red reflective safety vest, waving at us. He wants us to come forward.

We thread our way through the lines of cars and he halts the nearest vehicle and points us to the next empty inspection booth.

"Where are you going?" asks the young lady in the Customs uniform.

"Oakville, Ontario," I answer.

"How are you going to get there?" she asks.

"By bike. We've just ridden up from Virginia."

"Oh," she says, looking wide-eyed at me and then behind at Frank. "That explains your appearance."

Two other customs officers have now come over and joined her and a series of disjointed advice is being thrown at her, including another voice on her intercom. I have our passports in the saddlebags but she seems to have temporarily lost interest in us as she tries to sort out all the different suggestions.

I reckon we're in for a drug-busting strip search or some kind of intensive grilling but no. She doesn't ask what citizenship we have, where we're born, whether we have anything to declare ... none of the usual questions.

Instead, she picks up a waste paper basket, steps out of the little booth, followed by one of her colleagues carrying a chair, and they both summarily wave us through. It seems she's fairly new to the job and has never had bicyclists come through her lane. In fact, bicyclists don't usually come through anyone's lane. The experienced customs officials though are familiar with the problems that cyclists create and they're ready to assist her.

The real problem with cyclists is that we aren't big enough or heavy enough or high enough to trip any of the electronic sensors so the unseen alarm system won't deactivate when she presses her switch. One person has to block an electric eye with the waste paper basket and another has to reach up on the chair and reset some sort of switch.

"Have a good trip" she says good-naturedly and we move slowly forward. No bells. No sirens. No rush of Provincial Police.

She appears to have managed the trick of getting us through the border and, as I look around, I realize we have too.

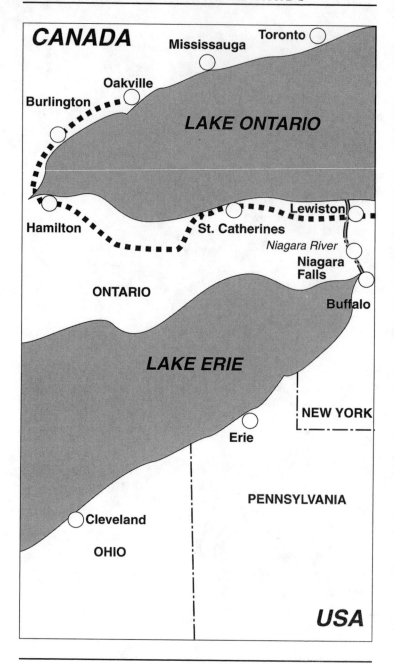

DAY 11
NIAGARA TO OAKVILLE

Last night we crossed the border just before dusk and headed west towards St. Catherines using a new Canadian Government army ordinance map sent to me by one of my brothers. The maps were detailed to the point of showing individual dwellings but they had almost no road names or numbers. Good enough, I concluded, for aerial bombing but not much good for navigating by bike as darkness fell.

We came down off Queenston Heights looking for one of the motels shown on the map but it was nowhere to be seen. When I stopped to ask directions a local told me the map must be way out of date. "Those motels have been gone for a long time," he said.

He recommended we push on for another five miles to a trucker's motel on the outskirts of St. Catherine's and see if someone there could help us. So we pushed on.

Just as darkness closed in us we spotted the huge neon Husky Truckstop sign and saw rank after rank of 18-wheelers parked alongside.

As we came into the restaurant I overheard a waitress at the counter explaining to a couple that there were no rooms available but they only had rooms for truckers anyway. I took off my helmet and put on my most appealing smile. I told her I realized there were no rooms but we had just bicycled up from Virginia and needed any kind of place to lay down. Told her we'd be willing to sleep in the lobby. Wouldn't mind just laying down outside if we could find a place we wouldn't be run over.

Told her that after 90 miles we didn't care where we slept but we just couldn't go on.

Exhaustion does strange things to your mental state. 'Though I am normally a model of veracity and integrity, I think I may actually have even told her that I was a trucker but had left my rig behind on this trip. It's possible I mentioned Jake Cochrane and Overnite Transportation. I really just put my mouth on automatic and let the words tumble out in a rush of pleading.

Another waitress overheard me and said "We're really don't have anything available. There's isn't a room left except of course No. 10 but the air conditioner doesn't work."

"Air conditioner?" I asked. "We don't need air conditioning. We live in Virginia and we don't even have air conditioning at home."

"Well, okay then," she said. "You can have No. 10."

Yahoo!

No Prime Minister of England was ever as grateful to get No. 10 as were that night. It was a small room without air conditioning but it had a shower and it had two big beds. It had room enough for us to wheel our bikes in. It had a window that opened and a door that closed. It had a roof. It was shelter.

Dinner was a blur — I remember huge portions and the waitress offering us second helpings. I must have had four or five cups of coffee. But the sleep: it was deep and unbroken and immediate.

Our last day's pedaling was almost all on the level. We cycled through Canada's famed Niagara Peninsula — the original fruit-growing region crisscrossed with dead-straight surveyors' grid roads dividing up orchards and vineyards, now being gobbled up by industries and housing tracts.

Mile after mile turned under us as we headed west along the Lakeshore Highway catching glimpses of Toronto's skyline across the lake. Traffic sped by on the 8-lane Queen Elizabeth Highway running parallel to us on the left but there was almost no traffic at all on the old road. Driving this road in the past I never realized how far west you have to travel before you round the end of Lake Ontario and can head east again on the north shore.

Just west of Jordan's Creek, watching waves pound on the shingle beach to our right, I saw the road taper, shift left and funnel into the QEW. It was unbelievable. It couldn't be.

I called a halt and looked first at out map and then at the road. There was no mistake. Some penny-pinching highway engineer had eliminated the Lakeshore Road across Jordan's Creek and all traffic went onto the one bridge and continued west for almost a quarter mile or more until old road shifted off again.

With my heart in my throat I told Frank to go ahead and I took up my blocking position 50 yards in his rear. Cars and trucks were tearing along at 70 to 80 miles an hour and all I could hope for was the care and courtesy of these harried foreign drivers.

It seemed like an hour but was probably less than five minutes later when we pulled off at the next exit and took a grateful breather. Standing astride our bikes and drinking from our water bottles we were hailed by two young men who came zipping toward us, passed us, turned back and pulled up beside us on the fanciest racing bikes I'd ever seen. They must have had $2000 worth of equipment each and they proudly proclaimed they had averaged a speed of 29.2 since leaving Oakville that morning headed for Niagara.

They were dressed in black nylon biking costumes with color-banded tops, molded stream-lined helmets, and told us their bikes weighed less than 11 pounds each.

"If you really want to appreciate what that means," I said, "try lifting this one," and I dismounted to let my bike stand free. One of the riders reached over and raised the front wheel a few inches but the rear wheel didn't budge. He tried again holding the seat and the cross bar but again couldn't raise it.

"My God," he said, his forearm bulging with the strain, "you must be pulling a hundred pounds!"

Well, not quite.

They wanted to know how we had crossed Jordan's Creek without having to go onto the QEW. We told them we hadn't and they were incredulous when we pointed back to the bridge and showed them that all traffic went on the QEW at that point. They decided they would walk their bikes down that stretch and remount when they were back on the old road. Wiser than us.

They also recommended we go up to Canada's "Heritage Highway" a few miles north and head east on that: a much more interesting road through the old farming communities and one that avoided all further contact with the QEW. It was excellent advice and a good road that took us through Hamilton, around Burlington Bay and back onto the Lakeshore Highway into Oakville.

Pedaling steadily on, about seven blocks from our final destination at my parent's house on the shore of Lake Ontario, we met two cars coming toward us with lights on, horns honking and streamers flapping out of the windows.

It was my mother, sister, brother, nephew, nieces — the whole family had decided to come out and greet us somewhere along the road and we had almost arrived before they set out. They turned around, passed us, pulled over and flagged us down to take pictures, cheering and hooray-ing at us as if we actually were on the Tour DuPont.

For some reason, it didn't seem much of an accomplishment to me. We hadn't got there yet. There was still another four blocks to go and my mind was thoroughly involved with the goal of getting there. I wouldn't be satisfied until I had actually pedaled into the driveway and dismounted onto somewhat wobbly legs, walked down the road, across the narrow parkway, down onto the stony beach and reached my hand into the water on the north shore of Lake Ontario.

We'd done it. This last day we traveled another 58 miles to my parents' house. It had taken us 11 days and we had ridden our bikes exactly 750.2 miles from our house in Virginia. Hard to believe but true.

"Wouldn't it be even more impressive in kilometers?" my sister asks.

Well, yes, I think to myself. That would be, let me see, multiply by eight, divide by five and you get ... 1200 kilometers. Yes. We've done 1200 kilometers in just 11 days.

Kilometers. Of course. That's how those two fellows near Jordan's Creek could average 29.2 — they were doing kilometers per hour. That would be about 18 miles per hour. Impressive. But we did 12 miles per hour on our trip today and we were carrying all that extra weight.

Still and all, looking out across Lake Ontario at the hazy outline of the Niagara Escarpment disappearing on the horizon I wondered more at the achievement of simply coming farther in one day than we could see over the curve of the earth's surface. I thought of the small boy back in Culpeper and wished he could see this. Miles and kilometers mean nothing when you can see something like this.

We came from down there, over the horizon, from Virginia, by bike, pedaling ... pedaling northwards.

Epilogue

THERE

W HEN I INSPECT MY BIKE for wear and tear I realize that I have replaced wheels, tubes and tires, wrist pins, brake pads, chain, free wheel sprockets, derailleur and the gear cable. I have come wobbling in without brakes, the rear wheel seriously out of balance, the right pedal grinding loosely on its shaft, most of the ballbearings somewhere back on the roadside. I discover four spokes have broken in the rather rough pounding of the last day along Canada's Heritage Highway. The front drive sprockets are sprung from the strain and the teeth are worn down from rubbing on the frame. My 21-year-old "restorable" — as the mechanic called in Pennsylvania — turned out to be an "old reliable" but I'm not sure there's much left original other than the frame. It did what was required of it.

I don't know how you go about honoring a bicycle but my initial reaction is to say "Nail this one to the wall. This is the one that got me to Canada in the summer of '93."

I recognize that some people might consider that too much an honor: after all, how can I go on the next adventure if the bike is permanently fixed to the wall? That's a very good question and it bears some study. I'm going to think about it long and hard — probably for the next several years at least. Right now everyone has questions. They want to know how we did it. Or why we did it. Or whether we'd do it again.

How did we stand up to the strain?

Well, I'm a little sunburned; my little fingers are numb from compressing my palms against the handlebars for such a long time, my knees are a little wobbly on the stairs, I've lost about 10 pounds and my chest has expanded two or three inches. Other than that I'm fine.

My 15 year-old son? I used to call him Frankie; now I call him 'Ironlegs'. He's sunburned and he's lost about five pounds. He says he wants to go round the world next summer. He's what I would call "fit." I reckon this summer vacation will stand him in good stead when his Cross Country team starts up in the fall.

And our experience together? What did we learn from all this sweaty bicycling? Will this help the transition between child and adult that we call being a teenager?

I don't know. I think that's a hill you just have to pedal up one turn after another. If you're responsible you'll look out for each other along the road. If you're lucky, your child waits for you to catch up. You learn to enjoy the downhill coasts when you get to them. (You realize you don't get downhill coasts until after the uphill strains.) You realize that the older the equipment, the more likely it is to suffer under pressure. You have to be prepared to repair or replace what gets strained and tired as the adventure unfolds. You spend a lot of time within sight of each other but unable to communicate. You learn to follow rather than lead. You remember, above all things, to always wear your helmet: you never know who's going to take a tumble or when.

Was it a bonding experience and would you do it again? Personally, I've always thought that people who wanted a bonding experience should go out and play with some Crazy Glue. As for my relation with young Ironlegs, I cannot imagine being more impressed with an exhibition of strength, endurance, independence, reliability, understanding and ..., yes, patience. I have learned a great deal about this up-and-coming new generation.

As to doing it again, I'll have to think about that after I find the nails to put this bicycle up on the wall.

If you Go

Bicycling is the process of going — not just getting there.

If you decide to take a bicycle trip there are plenty of things you will want to do in preparation. First, plan on setting aside time to plan.

When we were getting ready to set out I postponed our departure for several days until a heat wave passed — biking anywhere with temperatures at 100-degrees-plus is not only no fun but it can be seriously life-threatening. Don't risk it.

That delay proved to be a great boon because I was able to devote the extra time to planning the logistics for our trip — a process that I thought might take an hour or two turned into a two-day planning session that proved invaluable.

First, get your maps out and study the terrain: pick back roads wherever possible. (Remember, bicycling on Interstates is flatly prohibited, as well it ought to be. We built those monotonous highways to get the big trucks and fast cars off our roads and part of the deal is that we bikers don't get in their way.) After you've picked your route, try to break it into 50 to 60 mile stretches and find a suitable motel, bed & breakfast, former classmate or kinsman who can put you up for the night. Camping out is great, if you enjoy that sort of thing, but a hot shower is worth its weight in gold when you've pulled your weight up and downhill for 10 or 12 hours.

If you're a member of AAA get their tour books for the states you going through. Look up the areas along your route for places of interest, natural features, historical facts and local artifacts. (You'd kick yourself if you biked through Richmond and never heard of Monument Avenue, didn't know about the Poe House, Virginia Museum or Patrick Henry's speech at St. John's Church.)

Allow time for accidents, bad weather, equipment failures, getting lost, and — most of all — for enjoying the countryside. You don't want to be so pushed for reaching your destination that you don't have time to take in the sights and sounds, the interesting people and places you're going to come across. If you just want to be somewhere then you ought to drive or fly. We planned to spend fourteen days traveling to Canada and made it 750.2 miles in just 11 days. We were very lucky with the weather: only one day of rain and that was a light drizzle we were able to pedal through without hindrance.

Start with the best maps you can find. We used DeLorme's Gazetteer maps of Virginia, Maryland, Pennsylvania and New York and found them extraordinarily accurate and unfailingly detailed. They show every road, usually with both name and number, and all the natural features, including topography. (It's helpful to know if you're going to be going uphill or down and it saves a lot of time if you know that a high tension power line is crossing the valley just west of your next turnoff across a small creek.)

TIP: You don't have to take the whole map book with you. We cut out the pages that we needed and assembled them in our version of an AAA Trip-Tik. We then put them in a waterproof plastic baggie in our saddle bags and got out only the map we needed each day.

What to Take

The best rule of thumb is to assemble everything you think you'll need and then put half of it back. Remember: every item you put in your packs adds to the total pounds you have to push up those awful punishing hills.

We took three changes of clothes, each day's shirt, shorts, socks and smalls packed in a gallon-sized Zip-Loc bag. Wherever we went we never missed an opportunity to wash our clothes and when we were on our last day's kit we searched out a coin-op Laundromat and got everything clean again.

We also took an assortment of basic tools: screwdrivers, pliers, an adjustable wrench. Don't overdo it but don't fly naked thinking that there'll always be a bike shop nearby to fix whatever goes wrong. You ought to be able to jury-rig something to keep you going.

Most Important Equipment

The most important equipment we took was undoubtedly our bicycle helmets. I don't like 'em personally, prefer my old French beret, but I've seen the benefits and I'm sold on them; my beret is restricted now to my walking bouts.

The second most important piece of equipment I carried was the $3 nylon strap that kept my sunglasses from slipping down my nose. When you're riding and sweating and straining and looking up and down and around on unfamiliar roads, the last thing you need to do is reach up and push your glasses back into place 25 times an hour. And do wear glasses. You don't want to be enjoying a fast coast downhill around a blind corner and catch a eye full of dust, pollen, or grit.

Before You Go

I cannot emphasize enough the importance of having your equipment checked over by a competent mechanic. Believe me, I speak from painful experience.

Two of the mechanics in Richmond bike shops suggested I have my bike gone over before the trip and raised their eyebrows in surprise when I declined the advice. I knew better. I had used by bike off and on for 20 years and never had a bit of trouble. I wasn't going to waste my money on a boondoggle like that.

Well, 750 miles and almost $300 later I had learned my lesson. During the trip I discarded my broken tire pump and fractured kick stand, replaced my tires (four times), replaced both wheels, replaced the gear cable, pedal wrist pins, brake pads, chain, derailleur, and rear gears — and came in with no rear brakes, four broken spokes, the rear wheel wobbling out of alignment, and the right pedal grinding on its shaft without ball-bearings. My son's bike fared much better but a week after our return his front wheel collapsed about two miles from home when he was coasting down hill on a gentle right-hand-turn: the spokes simply worked loose and gave way, throwing him to the ground. He was all right but it could have been a fatal accident if it had happened when we were heavily laden and on the road in heavy traffic.

Don't Leave Home Without It

A major improvement in civilization over the past two decades is the development of plastic money card accepted by the now-ubiquitous Automated Teller Machines. I hate to carry cash of any amount and a cash card is a Godsend in foreign parts that might be reluctant to take your out-of-town check. In fact, if your card can stand the pressure, you have the luxury of being able to bicycle just about anywhere with nothing but your card: stay at motels or hotels and just sign for what your need as you go along.

TIP: If you're cycling with someone else make sure your companion knows the magic number for the card. When I first used mine in Troy, Pennsylvania I couldn't remember the Personal Identification Number; fortunately my 15-year-old came to my rescue and we soon had the cash we needed to proceed.

Water, Water, Water

When you're bicycling you're consuming fluids at an extraordinary rate. Those little water bottles you see on the bikes are essential. We took three quart bottles each and consumed about a quart an hour. Thirst is a trailing indicator of physiological stress; the general rule is that if you get thirsty, you're already in trouble.

We started out with Gatorade — the athletic drink that's supposed to restore "natural electrolytes" (as if you were a lead-acid battery of some kind) and it was the best thing I've ever tasted. We later switched to ice tea (the best I ever tasted) then plain water (the best I ever tasted) , then Coke, Pepsi, Ginger

Beer ... in fact, anything that was cold and wet and plentiful. Everything I drank provided a new level of satisfaction. Everything except alcohol. (I love a good drink and try to do my best to support government by consuming the heavily-taxed forms of liquid grains but not when I'm cycling. It's just not worth it. Ask your athletic director.)

Where to Stay

You can stay just about anywhere you would travelling by car: motel, hotel, bed & breakfast, friend or family. If you join the American Youth Hostel Association you can also stay very inexpensively ($8 a night) at their member hostels if there's one on your route. We carried bedrolls and were prepared to camp in state parks but ended up staying with family, friends, hostels and motels.

When you're travelling the back roads you will find your choices are limited and if you can't find a place to bed down before dark you're going to be in trouble. Please think ahead — *and Good Luck on your adventure!*

An audio casette of *"Pedaling Northwards"*, originally broadcast on WCVE-FM in Richmond, Virginia during November, 1993, is available for $9.95 plus $2 for shipping and handling from Hope Springs Press, P.O. Box 244, Manakin-Sabot, Virginia 23103.